**Self-portrait**

*The Getty Center for the History of Art and the Humanities, Los Angeles (Ca.)*

Towards the end of the 19th century Paris
changed in appearance ... l itself
... e
... his
... lt
... ffel
... 9
... ... impressionist
... ers fled from all this disturbance into
the countryside.

But not JEAN BÉRAUD. As a true city man he tried
with his pictures to capture the real vitality of urban
life, and so he walked the streets a great deal, along
the life-giving arteries of the French capital; from the
Champs-Elysées to Les Halles, from Montmartre to
the banks of the Seine. Even when he rode a coach,
he still kept his sketchbook out in order to capture
the tumult of the crowd with the vivacity of the
modern painter.

Béraud was a great observer of the public life of the
city as well as the worldly nightlife. He made portraits
of elegant society ladies – but also of working-class
women – and pictures of folk dancing and absinthe
drinkers in the bars and cafés. He took the same
interest in the everyday business of living as he did
in great historical events.

Béraud was one of the best chroniclers of the Belle
Epoque and this picture selection not only invites you
to discover a great artist's work, but also guides you
back to the Paris of a long-vanished era – a journey
of nostalgia.

**Jean Béraud**
*Bibliothèque Nationale de France, Paris*

Gegen Ende des 19. Jahrhunderts veränderte Paris sein Gesicht und schmückte sich mit den Emblemen der Moderne. Georges Haussmann hatte seine breiten Boulevards angelegt, Charles Garnier baute die prunkvolle Oper und Gustave Eiffel seinen Turm als Wahrzeichen der Weltausstellung im Jahre 1889. Viele Maler, vor allem die Impressionisten, flohen diesen Trubel und zogen aufs Land. Nicht so JEAN BÉRAUD. Als eingefleischter Stadtmensch will er mit seinen Bildern die Lebendigkeit des Urbanen festhalten, und so flaniert er unermüdlich über die Boulevards, die Lebensadern der französischen Hauptstadt, von den Champs-Elysées zu Les Halles, vom Montmartre zu den Quais der Seine. Selbst wenn er in der Kutsche fährt, legt Béraud seinen Skizzenblock nicht aus der Hand.

Béraud erweist sich sowohl als genauer Beobachter des regen Treibens auf den Boulevards als auch der mondänen Abendgesellschaften; er porträtiert die Damen der eleganten Welt, aber auch geschäftige Arbeiterinnen, volkstümliche Tanzvergnügungen und Absinthtrinker in verräucherten Cafés. Zweifelsohne war Jean Béraud einer der begabtesten Chronisten der Belle Epoque; den vielfältigen Erscheinungen des Pariser Alltagslebens widmete er das gleiche Interesse wie zahlreichen historischen Ereignissen.

Diese Auswahl führt zurück in das Paris einer lang vergangenen Epoche und lädt dazu ein, Bérauds großes malerisches Œuvre zu entdecken.

**Jean Béraud**: Une soirée, 1878
Soirée
Oil on canvas, 65.1 x 116.8 cm. Paris, Musée d'Orsay
© 1999 VG Bild-Kunst, Bonn
*Also reproduced in:* JEAN BÉRAUD. THE BELLE ÉPOQUE: A DREAM
OF TIMES GONE BY, Benedikt Taschen Verlag

TASCHEN

Jean Béraud. 1889

**Jean Béraud**: La Sortie du bourgeois, 1889
The Bourgeois Steps Out
Oil on panel, 37.5 x 53 cm. Private collection
© 1999 VG Bild-Kunst, Bonn
*Also reproduced in:* JEAN BÉRAUD. THE BELLE ÉPOQUE: A DREAM
OF TIMES GONE BY, Benedikt Taschen Verlag

TASCHEN

**Jean Béraud**: Boulevard des Capucines
Boulevard des Capucines
Oil on canvas, 51 x 73 cm. Private collection
© 1999 VG Bild-Kunst, Bonn
*Also reproduced in:* JEAN BÉRAUD. THE BELLE ÉPOQUE: A DREAM
OF TIMES GONE BY, Benedikt Taschen Verlag

**TASCHEN**

**Jean Béraud:** Le Chalet du cycle au bois de Boulogne
The Chalet du Cycle in the Bois de Boulogne
Oil on panel, 53.5 x 65 cm. Paris, Musée Carnavalet
© 1999 VG Bild-Kunst, Bonn
*Also reproduced in:* JEAN BÉRAUD. THE BELLE ÉPOQUE: A DREAM
OF TIMES GONE BY, Benedikt Taschen Verlag

**TASCHEN**

**Jean Béraud:** Autour du piano
Around the Piano
Oil on panel, 35 x 27 cm. Paris, Musée Carnavalet
© 1999 VG Bild-Kunst, Bonn
Also *reproduced in:* JEAN BÉRAUD. THE BELLE ÉPOQUE: A DREAM
OF TIMES GONE BY, Benedikt Taschen Verlag

**TASCHEN**

**Jean Béraud**: *Scène de bistrot*
At the Bistro
Oil on panel, 46 x 38 cm. Private collection
© 1999 VG Bild-Kunst, Bonn
*Also reproduced in:* JEAN BÉRAUD. THE BELLE ÉPOQUE: A DREAM
OF TIMES GONE BY, Benedikt Taschen Verlag

**TASCHEN**

**Jean Béraud**: Le Pont des Arts par grand vent
Pont des Arts: Windy Day
Oil on panel, 17.5 x 26 cm. Private collection
© 1999 VG Bild-Kunst, Bonn
*Also reproduced in:* JEAN BÉRAUD. THE BELLE ÉPOQUE: A DREAM
OF TIMES GONE BY, Benedikt Taschen Verlag

**TASCHEN**

**Jean Béraud:** Un *Figaro de rêve*
Daydream with *Figaro*
Oil on canvas, 65 x 54.3 cm. Private collection
© 1999 VG Bild-Kunst, Bonn
*Also reproduced in:* JEAN BÉRAUD. THE BELLE ÉPOQUE: A DREAM
OF TIMES GONE BY, Benedikt Taschen Verlag

TASCHEN

**Jean Béraud**: Entrée de l'Exposition universelle de 1889
Entrance to the 1889 Universal Exhibition
Oil on panel, 30 x 40 cm. Paris, Musée Carnavalet
© 1999 VG Bild-Kunst, Bonn
*Also reproduced in:* JEAN BÉRAUD. THE BELLE ÉPOQUE: A DREAM
OF TIMES GONE BY, Benedikt Taschen Verlag

**TASCHEN**

**Jean Béraud**: Femme au café
Woman in a Café
Oil on canvas, 52 x 46 cm. Paris, Musée des Arts décoratifs
© 1999 VG Bild-Kunst, Bonn
*Also reproduced in:* JEAN BÉRAUD. THE BELLE ÉPOQUE: A DREAM
OF TIMES GONE BY, Benedikt Taschen Verlag

**TASCHEN**

**Jean Béraud:** Paris, la rue du Havre
Paris, Rue du Havre
Oil on canvas, 35.3 x 27.3 cm. Washington D. C., National Gallery of Art
© 1999 VG Bild-Kunst, Bonn
*Also reproduced in:* JEAN BÉRAUD. THE BELLE ÉPOQUE: A DREAM
OF TIMES GONE BY, Benedikt Taschen Verlag

**TASCHEN**

Jean Béraud

**Jean Béraud:** Devant la tour Eiffel
Near the Eiffel Tower
Oil on panel, 46 x 29.5 cm. Paris, Musée des Arts décoratifs
© 1999 VG Bild-Kunst, Bonn
*Also reproduced in:* JEAN BÉRAUD. THE BELLE ÉPOQUE: A DREAM
OF TIMES GONE BY, Benedikt Taschen Verlag

**TASCHEN**

**Jean Béraud:** Le Secret
The Secret
Oil on canvas, 35 x 27 cm, Paris, Musée des Arts décoratifs
© 1999 VG Bild-Kunst, Bonn
*Also reproduced in:* Jean Béraud. The Belle Époque: A Dream
of Times Gone By, Benedikt Taschen Verlag

**TASCHEN**

**Jean Béraud**: La Porte Saint-Denis
Porte Saint-Denis
Oil on canvas, 37 x 55 cm. Private collection
© 1999 VG Bild-Kunst, Bonn
*Also reproduced in*: JEAN BÉRAUD. THE BELLE ÉPOQUE: A DREAM
OF TIMES GONE BY, Benedikt Taschen Verlag

**TASCHEN**

**Jean Béraud**: La Marseillaise, 1880
The Marseillaise
Oil on canvas, 38 x 55 cm. Private collection
© 1999 VG Bild-Kunst, Bonn
*Also reproduced in:* JEAN BÉRAUD. THE BELLE ÉPOQUE: A DREAM
OF TIMES GONE BY, Benedikt Taschen Verlag

**TASCHEN**

**Jean Béraud**: La Baignoire, 1883
The Ground-Floor Box
Oil on canvas, 49 x 40 cm. Paris, Musée Carnavalet
© 1999 VG Bild-Kunst, Bonn
*Also reproduced in:* JEAN BÉRAUD. THE BELLE ÉPOQUE: A DREAM
OF TIMES GONE BY, Benedikt Taschen Verlag

**TASCHEN**

**Jean Béraud**: Dîner aux Ambassadeurs
Dinner at the Ambassadeurs
Oil on panel, 35.5 x 45.5 cm. Paris, Musée Carnavalet
© 1999 VG Bild-Kunst, Bonn
*Also reproduced in:* JEAN BÉRAUD. THE BELLE ÉPOQUE: A DREAM
OF TIMES GONE BY, Benedikt Taschen Verlag

TASCHEN

**Jean Béraud**: Revue du théâtre des Variétés
The Revue at the Théâtre des Variétés
Oil on canvas, 46.5 x 38.5 cm. Paris, Musée des Arts décoratifs
© 1999 VG Bild-Kunst, Bonn
*Also reproduced in:* Jean Béraud. The Belle Époque: A Dream
of Times Gone By, Benedikt Taschen Verlag

TASCHEN

**Jean Béraud**: La Proposition
The Proposition
Oil on panel, 55 x 38 cm, Paris, Musée des Arts décoratifs
© 1999 VG Bild-Kunst, Bonn
*Also reproduced in:* JEAN BÉRAUD. THE BELLE ÉPOQUE: A DREAM
OF TIMES GONE BY, Benedikt Taschen Verlag

**TASCHEN**

Jean Béraud

**Jean Béraud:** Jeune Femme traversant le boulevard
Young Woman Crossing the Boulevard
Oil on panel, 52 x 35.7 cm. Private collection
© 1999 VG Bild-Kunst, Bonn
*Also reproduced in:* JEAN BÉRAUD. THE BELLE ÉPOQUE: A DREAM
OF TIMES GONE BY, Benedikt Taschen Verlag

TASCHEN

**Jean Béraud**: Sur le boulevard
On the Boulevard
Oil on canvas, 53.5 x 37.5 cm, Stockton (Ca.), The Haggin Museum
© 1999 VG Bild-Kunst, Bonn
*Also reproduced in:* Jean Béraud. The Belle Époque: A Dream
of Times Gone By, Benedikt Taschen Verlag

TASCHEN

**Jean Béraud**: Le Boulevard des Capucines et le théâtre du Vaudeville, 1889
Boulevard des Capucines and Théâtre du Vaudeville
Oil on panel, 35 x 51 cm, Paris, Musée Carnavalet
© 1999 VG Bild-Kunst, Bonn
*Also reproduced in:* JEAN BÉRAUD. THE BELLE ÉPOQUE: A DREAM
OF TIMES GONE BY, Benedikt Taschen Verlag

**TASCHEN**

Jean Béraud

**Jean Béraud**: Parisienne, place de la Concorde
Parisienne, Place de la Concorde
Oil on panel, 35 x 26 cm, Paris, Musée Carnavalet
© 1999 VG Bild-Kunst, Bonn
*Also reproduced in:* JEAN BÉRAUD, THE BELLE ÉPOQUE: A DREAM
OF TIMES GONE BY, Benedikt Taschen Verlag

TASCHEN

**Jean Béraud**: Vue de l'avenue des Champs-Elysées
View of the Champs-Elysées
Oil on panel, 55 x 73 cm, Paris, Musée des Arts décoratifs
© 1999 VG Bild-Kunst, Bonn
*Also reproduced in*: Jean Béraud. The Belle Époque: A Dream
of Times Gone By, Benedikt Taschen Verlag

**TASCHEN**

Jean Béraud

**Jean Béraud:** Jeune Femme à l'éventail

Young Lady with a Fan

Oil on panel, 22 x 14 cm. Private collection

© 1999 VG Bild-Kunst, Bonn

Also *reproduced in:* JEAN BÉRAUD. THE BELLE ÉPOQUE: A DREAM
OF TIMES GONE BY, Benedikt Taschen Verlag

TASCHEN

**Jean Béraud:** Jeune Fille au parasol japonais au bord de la Seine
Young Girl with Japanese Parasol on the Banks of the Seine
Oil on canvas, 65 x 54 cm. Charlieu (France), Société des Amis
des Arts de Charlieu
© 1999 VG Bild-Kunst, Bonn
*Also reproduced in:* JEAN BÉRAUD. THE BELLE ÉPOQUE: A DREAM
OF TIMES GONE BY, Benedikt Taschen Verlag

**TASCHEN**

**Jean Béraud:** La Sortie des ouvrières de la maison Paquin
Dressmakers Leaving Maison Paquin
Oil on panel, 42 x 55 cm. Paris, Musée Carnavalet
© 1999 VG Bild-Kunst, Bonn
*Also reproduced in:* JEAN BÉRAUD. THE BELLE ÉPOQUE: A DREAM
OF TIMES GONE BY, Benedikt Taschen Verlag

TASCHEN

**Jean Béraud:** Jeune Femme, rond-point des Champs-Elysées sous la neige
Young Woman, Rond-Point des Champs-Elysées, Snow
Watercolour, 41 x 34.5 cm. Private collection
© 1999 VG Bild-Kunst, Bonn
*Also reproduced in:* JEAN BÉRAUD. THE BELLE ÉPOQUE: A DREAM
OF TIMES GONE BY, Benedikt Taschen Verlag

TASCHEN

Jean Béraud, 1889

**Jean Béraud**: La Pâtisserie Gloppe, 1889
Pâtisserie Gloppe
Oil on panel, 38 x 53 cm, Paris, Musée Carnavalet
© 1999 VG Bild-Kunst, Bonn
Also *reproduced in*: JEAN BÉRAUD. THE BELLE ÉPOQUE: A DREAM
of TIMES GONE BY, Benedikt Taschen Verlag

TASCHEN

**Jean Béraud**: La Sortie du lycée Condorcet
Leaving Lycée Condorcet
Oil on canvas, 51 x 65 cm. Paris, Musée Carnavalet
© 1999 VG Bild-Kunst, Bonn
*Also reproduced in:* Jean Béraud. The Belle Époque: A Dream
of Times Gone By, Benedikt Taschen Verlag

**TASCHEN**